I0840164

The Path to Peace

Poems for the Willing Heart

Renée C. Harp

reneeharpstudios.com

The Path to Peace

Trust the perfect timing...
we weren't who we are until now

Preface - Notes on the process

The verses come differently from the writing I do every day. They come thorough me, without the option for me to choose the words, or even to edit them very much. They insist on their words and structure. It is a frightening risk for me to put them out in the world, without wrapping them in my comfortable academic wordiness, well-edited for anything anyone could critique.

But this is not their job, to be unobjectionable. And I am clear they do not come to me for my benefit. And I do not get to sleep until I put them out. This is the third time I have had this experience, and still I have no way to make sense of it. I am unable to resist the need to preface this body of verse with my perspective. I am passionate about the possibility of seeing more harmony between humans in my lifetime. I don't feel terribly hopeful about that timing, but I know one thing about myself; it is not optional that I be a part of the trying.

These sixteen verse are part exploration of idealistic impossibility, and part glimpse into the process of wrestling with burning desire to be a part of evolution as a species. Some verse have their rose-colored glasses firmly in place, like a beacon into an impossible fantasy. Some stare down the heart-breaking dilemma of humans who would love to love each other, if only we could still get our way. Some of them hint to you of the rightness of your position, as if you and I are on the same side; but it wouldn't matter what "side" you were on, you would hear the same message from me.

It is a wondrous magical trick, that the human mind can dwell on two levels of a problem at the same time. I can see the dichotomy, I can see the opposing views, I have my own, and I can still see how the "other side" is not crazy or bad, any more than I am. I can see your pain, which breaks my heart.

It is my earnest, almost wrenching desire, that my description of inner wrestling is able to help someone else make that bizarre nonsensical leap to being able to see both sides, whatever the issue may be.

And still some other verse are a glimpse behind the veil, the inner process of writing, an offering of my own struggle, so as to be utterly clear that I am not proposing a virtuous moral ground that I have attained. I am standing at the foot of this mountain, aspiring with most of humanity, for the summit, or even just a scenic overlook, where the view is just a little less heavy than this one, today, as 2020 gives way to 2021.

I have wished nearly my whole life for articulate enough words to inspire a generation. I am fame-phobic, so the fantasy is just that, detached from reality. But if my words are part of a growing chorus, and there are those who take up the hope and put it in words that do reach large groups of people, then I will have done what I could.

I will just go for it, and wonder out loud, what could 2022 look like, if a widespread movement of tolerance and understanding and compassion and acceptance and empathy (love in action, in other words) swept across the country, the world, in an unbelievable wave of trendiness?

I will not stop dreaming of that day.

Renée

Renée Christine Harp
January 30, 2021

If We Did

If we all agreed toward love

Amidst the roar of this and that

Nothing more to agree upon
BUT NOTHING LESS

and surely we do?
agree?444
on that?
?

and what a relief to simply let go of not agreeing
about
any
thing
else

what a relief
so much it brings tears to my eyes

because I CANNOT sort it all out
I can't prove all of mine, or make sense of all of yours

I try

But I cannot, will not, ever,

be able to be okay with everything you present

AND BE CLEAR... i can't even be okay with
all of me

and now, more than ever, i don't know for sure…

ANYTHING AT ALL

except this…

it is at least
possible
we all could agree
on love

(each to their own definition, of course)

but moving in that direction

What If We Did

And what if we did?
oh i know
we can't really
agree

even if we did, secretly

it is too important not to
agree

but,

and just pretend I am your 6 year old in the backseat
of a too long trip

but what if we did?
what if we did?

ok, but what if we did?

(because secretly i think we do)

so what if we agreed that we did…
agree?

oh. my. goodness.

the hair on the back of my neck just stood up, all of it,
as I wrote
(because I don't know what is coming next
until each word appears)

BUT WHAT IF WE DID??????

just admit that there might be one thing we could all
(most of us, anyway)

AGREE ON

...and just agree not to
define it
argue about it
explore
the nuances
ramifications
enforcement
risk
cost
humbling IMPLICATIONS

and just rested
for a brief moment
in the never-before-experienced
reality
of something we could all imagine agreeing upon

just that experience, lasting 2.7 seconds

it would change the world

OK, So Seriously, What WOULD Happen

(remember, I'm 6)

What if we really did?
What if you did?

Right
I have to set that down, let that go, release any need
for anyone else to do anything

what if I did

agree

with whom?

I agree with anyone who might be currently in the
position to agree

that imagining us all agreeing
on love
conceptually

just that act, of imagining us all already wanting to
moving generally in the direction of more love

(and i will just have to not worry about the
troublesome fact that there will always be those who
actually do not want that for themselves)

IS A REVOLUTION

Because it is a revolutionary concept

to imagine, without requiring evidence of participation

that we are all wanting the same thing,
at the most primal level

an okay-ness with our life, self, others, world, reality

that has a shared quality
even while being made up of very different criteria

But here's the wonderment,
what happens to ME if i allow myself to believe
that everyone i see and hear
just wants the same thing?
the same basic profound all-encompassing state of
IT'S ALL GOOD

defined differently
but experienced nonetheless as a state of being that
we all recognize

and if i give it a name,
so i can hold it in my mind's eye,
i have no need for you to give it the same name

because again, the curiosity is…
What happens to ME if i see everyone wanting the
same thing?

Really?

Am I the only one who traveled in a car
for hours
with children?

"ok ok ok ok, but WHAT IF IT DID?"

my favorite version of this game was…

"Would you drink my spit?"
"If I was dying, and it would save my life, would you
drink my spit?"
"BUT NO REALLY, IF I REALLY WAS DYING, AND IT
REALLY WOULD SAVE MY LIFE???"

The game had many versions, but the point was, that
you had to

ACCEPT A PREMISE FIRST
without arguing about its existence
or ridiculousness

So that's the deal.…

I know it is not possible
beyond the realm of imaginable, in fact
that humans would agree

that even two people would agree
very far down the road
on anything

so bear with me

WHAT IF WE DID

what do you think might happen?

somehow I think it is in the imagining of that
preposterous scenario
that there is
somewhere in there
a piece of magic miraculous unrealistic truth

that has the power

all the power

Suspend Reality

Question the value of good reality testing

Ok that did not go where I thought it was going
And that's okay

What fun
anyway
to play

with words
with what happens after the words
the magic of the words themselves

an exercise in suspending insistence on reality being
what i know it to be

and good grief, nobody seems very happy with reality
these days anyway

those who seem to have mastered something
        or paradoxically, given up
        on mastering anything,
        and surrendered to
        the saving grace of that failure
don't put much stock in reality
as it is described

or even in the existence of reality

and most of us know that two people at the same car
accident, standing in the same place, can't even
agree on basic details

the colors of the clothing the people were wearing

which would seem like a verifiable fact

oh how we humans hate to think we don't have the
market cornered on reality-testing
ours, that is

but in this thought experiment
i wonder

        what if it's much worse than we suspected?

        what if I am MUCH worse at correctly defining
            WHAT'S WHAT than I ever dreamed?

        what if I'm so wrong, so far off, that seeing my
            error would make me throw up?

I've had that experience, haven't you?
…the horrifying realization that something was so
very different from what I thought, that my actions
were regrettable beyond my ability to cope with the
shock/shame/regret

What if my whole perspective on life with humans is
just that far off?

I guess I had to come this far with some degree of
certainty about SOME things, just to be strong
enough to survive being that wrong. So I can forgive
myself for past certainty.

…and wonder if I am strong enough now to entertain
the possibility that i actually don't know anything?

**A digression that I trust will somehow tie
in, as it will not allow further movement
forward until acknowledged**

What if I am writing just to get attention?
That is why i keep most of it secret

what a dilemma

write
hide it write more
wonder if I should
share
get excited
take that as confirmation that ego is running the show
don't share

years

and then that poke
nudge

YOU ARE NOT GOING TO BE PERMITTED
ANY SLEEP
UNTIL YOU DO SOMETHING

then, words i don't usually publish, or say to anyone
more not sleeping
more of the sort of words i would never put in print
more not sleeping

and this time i recognize it sooner

just put it out

then let it go

ego is just as invested in praise as it is in criticism,
and even more caught up in
getting something, anything,
rather than
nothing

so risk the possibility of
nothing
risk the dangers of praise that feels so good
it's undeniably bad for me
risk criticism, which has its own rewards to the ego
risk nothing happening at all,
which is death
to the ego

and isn't that what i want anyway?
…release from the cruel requirements of ego

maybe hiding is just the protection of grandiosity
holding on to the hope that
greatness
is still out in front of me

so i reject all of it
no, wait
that's still too invested, too forceful

i wish to be always aware that none of it matters
to me

because it isn't supposed to

What Would Happen If

I wish I could make it all make sense
express something with the certainty that it hangs
together towards a goal

but that is the point

i am not the author, or at least the sole author
and so it is the height of arrogance to question

as if i know better

as if my critical rational logical analytical educated left
brain is somehow the answer that anyone needs

as if

Because love
which i happen to know IS the answer,
and this is the sum total of everything I know for a fact

is in no way rational.
or logical.
it does not make sense
strategically

it is no part of an MBA course

it can't be taught
it can't be prescribed
it can't be sold, advertised, promoted

i can't even tell you what it is

But every language, every time, every civilization,
every body of cultural remnants…

recognizes a pointing in the direction
of
the
same
thing

       yes, experienced differently
       I will honor that every time

but still

what if we all agreed that there is SOME ONE THING
that we all
already
agree on

I'm not saying that's true.

But I'm six, and I'm saying, what would happen if we
agreed that it was?

feelings are not points on a compass

it's just flowing, and i don't go back and re-read
and i kinda desperately want to make sure it all
makes sense, feel an urgency for it to

which i know it doesn't
and I'm mostly okay with that

but i feel urgency
frantic
boiling
agitated with the utter desperate certainty of someone
as far from an ocean of peace as you can get
not sleeping must not wait til it's all pretty and perfect
my life depends on it urgency

to say something that's already been said
a million times
and me having no new words to say it with

but let me try, if only to sleep tonight…

I am a solid 45 years into intentionally reaching for
understanding/peace/trust/compassion/optimism/faith
and in most ways i can see, i have less of all of the
above than I did in fourth grade, when I believed that
at least all of that was going to be possible, if I worked
really really hard at it.

And now, with a solid 35 years of therapy
(both ends of the couch)
I believe
more than ever

in the importance of acceptance
of everyone
on their own terms

possibly it is my only solid take-away

too many confirmations of my inability
to know what is best for anyone else

too many experiences of the
annihilating
power of judgment and condemnation and rejection
from others

so I believe
in acceptance
as the non-negotiable bare minimum requirement
without which,
nothing
nothing else matters

and at the exact same time, I feel less of it than ever

guessing I'm not alone
guessing that's not because I'm evil
or broken
guessing
that's just the way it is

that this belief in acceptance
which I have put everything on the line for,
has nothing to do with my feelings
or how utterly dismayed i was yesterday at what
a human is capable of

feelings are not points on a compass

So love, then

A decision to practice acceptance
not tolerance
but acceptance

the belief that
if practiced

well. then maybe nothing is attained
except being in a state of practicing

and that beats being in a state of practicing
something else

as a matter of fact
it certainly appears
that a significant number of humans
put a significant number of hours
into the practice
of hate

a cover for fear, jealousy, insecurity, injustice,
resentment, despair
lack of hope for anything to change

so i can understand that
can't fix it
not one bit of it

except to practice the antidote

not sure

Not sure there is anything more to say
actually, sure there isn't

WHICH HAS NEVER STOPPED ME BEFORE
But all I've got is:

I know our differences are mostly irreconcilable
because

and this is the kicker

we need them to be.

Knowing   what we are not
               who is not with us
               what we are against

IS

how we know ourselves.

And that is what i insist on doing differently

that is why, to the best of my ability,
and currently to the best of my knowledge

I have resisted the temptation to stridently point out
my utterly defensible
outrage

anywhere

publicly

which is not to say
I don't have plenty of outrage
which must be processed, evaluated, resolved,
channeled, transcended, transmuted, translated,
harnessed,
sometimes after much venting
sometimes
much

just this:

i have many lovely things
in my personal mission statement,

but only one thing that matters

Only one test for what I say and do
and that is to always flip my feelings
whatever they are
into what I am FOR

and this little trick, it is everything

For

such an easy thing
what do I want
what do I really want to stand FOR?

And why is "no" one of the first words we learn?
no is easy

knowing is much, much harder

I can say no to pain
quite easily

knowing what I must say yes to instead
to change the pain
much harder
and requiring action

no is a feeling
and it is a good one

yes is footsteps
and I'd rather netflix and chill
no self-defining required
no discernement
no outrageous openness
no embracing uncertainty

none of those awful books
that touch my heart and wrench it around
and give me less answers
and more certainty
that THIS life

THIS life, is not about answers or fixing pain

but we mustn't stop trying

sorry to end on a paradox

Love is a non-optional craziness

Love just makes no sense
but everything else that isn't of love
even the good stuff
the reasonably responsible stuff

once disconnected from a commitment to love others

quickly snowballs

restless
ennui
craving
something
disconcerting feeling of missing
something

a lack of enough meaning, even where there is some
meaning
because the attainment of even the worthiest goal

is just so empty
alone

and together
requires
a special kind of crazy

the crazy notion
that you
as wrong as you look to me
or as right as you look to me
are essential to me

and that your wrongness doesn't negate that

but neither does your rightness
(the comfort i feel when you validate my values)
defend it

you are essential
because
that is the way the game is set up

and the sooner i get on board with that,
with actually accepting you,
regardless of all the ways you
comfort and discomfort me
the sooner I become

part of the solution
to the problem that is never to be solved

Trying to accomplish something

I keep wanting to pile on more words
not to convince you
maybe to convince me?
but no

more words,

because no matter how many
no matter how pretty
or delightfully sharp

they just don't ever get the job done

why poets?

hasn't it all been said?
and isn't it all pretty much the same thing
over the hundreds of years?

but we must
speak
write
read
hear

it is compelling to nearly everyone
at some time

words
in an attempt to get a handle on this swirling mass
inside of me

in an attempt to get it out of me
to put it in order
to be understood
to reach
someone

and there it is

the words, that I know are just a practice,
are essentially in service of the very thing I keep
trying to define

to reach someone

and what is that, if not the purest form of just me,
as I am,
making contact with just you,
as you are,
with both of us being okay enough
in the being seen

seen accurately.

known.

and and what is that, if not the definition of love

How would we know?

worlds apart
and occupying the same existential reality
for all of millennia

never ending
never finishing
only love

the ultimate infinite

call it whatever you want

i think we all already agree
-with a different set of words for every single human

and groups of humans who
agree to agree
on certain words
which is a beautiful thing

and then of course, there are all the other humans
who don't
agree to agree
on those same words
they're wrong

and so just within this space of writing, I must
withdraw my argument
that agreeing
is good

as we can't seem to do it

without
quickly
and alarmingly

attempting to punish those who don't

so I won't start a new club
with a better, more all-encompassing word

I will just wonder
a brand new curiosity just this second

what if we were not able to use any words,
had none,
or couldn't,
or they simply did not exist?

how would we know who disagreed with us?
failed to agree that we really all do
want the same thing
but would we please use my word for it

how would we know who was wrong?
how would we know who to hate?

Stepping out of the dance

Just when I think I'm empty

because i suspect
i am

and this is not wholly my truth
or else i would be recognized
as some kind of saint
or at least a legit famous person
or at the very least a poet of instagram

NOT

…and i want to be very clear about this

not because i find myself so articulate
or even brilliant or delightful

but because
if this was just me writing *my* thoughts
i would be alot more at peace

i would BE these words
and that much acceptance
down to the bones
would be notable

because it is a rare thing

the truth is, I am not these words
down to my bones

i agree with them
wholeheartedly

but i fail to live them

every day i fail

in truth, i am failing most of the time

run by fear of the future,
and resentment about the past,
and mostly
that as much as I hope
and try to trust

it just might not be enough
for me
for me to ever feel the peace that it looks like "they"
have found
in their release of attachments

I am still very attached
I am still so very very attached

to the people I love
to the poignancy of past experiences that are no more
to the fear of loss

to…

the blinding despair I feel

when something that could be so joyful and playful
and easy and fun
apparently cannot be
apparently can never be

apparently our human condition will always compel us
to stand against whatever we think stands against our
happiness and peace

another paradox

    if I resist what hurts me, I add to the hurt
    victimhood is not an option
    stopping someone else is never an option
    can't stop it, can't fight it, can't submit to it

        must
        must transcend

the only answer to the unsolvable problem

                autocorrect changed that to
                "the unlovable problem"
                three times
                …a curiosity for another time

the only answer to the unsolvable problem is to
transcend it

the answer not being a solution, but an action
unrelated to the source of problem

What is unrelated to injury?

What is unrelated to feeling like a helpless victim?

What is unrelated to outrage at injustice?

What is not attached to making anything outside of my self operate differently?

Only choosing what I am FOR

A lovable problem

"the unlovable problem"

a curiosity for now

so this is what i do
having nothing in my mind to say
nevertheless
starting to write
because
well i don't really know…

This has all been on the agenda of love as the answer

     to a problem that is unlovable???

no, i think it is that we are
supposed to love this problem too

what is the problem here?
pain and suffering
their inherent unsolvablilty

the rejection of that problem simply causing more of it
the paralysis we got stuck in by that
seeming paradox:

     I must resist bad things,
     and thereby I create more negativity
     more no's
     more judgement
     more censure, punishment, pain and suffering
     I create more of the bad things I must resist

Familiar setup. Familiar solution.
I didn't invent love
or the preaching of love as the answer

But this last slip, it says
THE PROBLEM ITSELF COULD BE LOVED

after all, if something can be *not loved*, it can *be loved*
and i *am* proposing acceptance of all that is
(also not an original thought)

But this is a conundrum
love the problem itself
love the problem of pain and suffering begetting hate
and violence begetting more pain and suffering
begetting more hate and violence.
Which is to be condemned.
And not at all tolerated as acceptable behavior.
Love THAT

And thus another what if, that is not
in the slightest way
appealing,
but intriguing

Love that problem itself
I have no idea what that would mean

What is to be gained?

A ground,
against which the figure of love
is so beautiful it compels

Really? that's it?
could it be?

Conclusion

Conclusion - Notes on a paradox

A paradox is an interesting phenomenon. Two incompatible essential Truths. A chain of cause and effect with no start, and no end, which nonetheless must be interrupted. Diametrically opposed needs, each mandatory, each destroying the other, but existing in the same one person, or one system.

At turns frustrating, but just as possibly a delight to the child-like mind some of us are working our way back to. And in that frame of mind, a paradox offers the possibility of transcendence... a third position in which the previous two incompatible problem-states simply cease to matter. An observing perspective, in which the determination of cause and effect, blame and responsibility, is simply abandoned. The desire to determine right and wrong is released, not because that feels like an acceptable solution, just because continuing to cling to it will make losers of us all. The problem of the paradox is not solved, it is simply out-grown as a valid definition. Something new, some radical new perspective, is entered into without trying to make sense of how it is the solution; it is simply a better way to be.

Trapped in a paradox as a culture, humans take sides and emotionally commit to right and wrong, to the impossibility of seeing the others as humans with a valid perspective. Our side is so clearly right and good, theirs so clearly wrong and bad. And oh how committed we are. How entrenched we become in the belief that the only solution is the defeat of the enemy. How utterly impossible it seems that we could release ANYTHING without a sense of resolution.

The escape from this requires some of us to simply be unwilling to continue on those terms. We don't have to resolve the points of disagreement; they aren't resolvable. That is why we are stuck. We can have resolution, or we can have revolution. We cannot have both.

The only reason to escape from this deadly trap is that I for one do not want to fight to the death. I don't want to abandon my values, and I don't want to inflict pain and suffering on anyone else, but I can't see a resolution to the differences either. I only know for sure this one thing: a commitment to conflict ultimately destroys us all, robs us all of any quality of life, of every good thing, except for righteous indignation. Am I willing to sacrifice EVERYTHING for the satisfaction of righteous indignation? Sadly, yes, I am, on too many days. But on those few days when I am tapped into something that is bigger than me, better and more generous than my mortal humanity, I am more than willing to lay it down. I am desperately eager to reinforce the tiny fragile bud of desire to truly love everyone, regardless of their values, and enter that glorious realm of possibility.

I am a pragmatic realist enough to know I can't stay in this state of mind. Too well acquainted with humanity to think we could all achieve this state of delight in our differences, in the end of fighting, in a common commitment to help each other enjoy this life of infinite possibilities.

And yet, there is this part of me that will not let go of the dream. Even if it is a fantasy, on the days I allow it to be where I dwell in my thoughts and feelings, I know this is heaven on earth.

I will probably not be dissuaded of the belief that this is what everyone ultimately wants. I think the most cynical of us still would prefer fun, happy, joy, love, peace, delight in ourselves and each other. That is my belief. I think we want to be happy. I think we want to get along. I think we just don't trust that we can, without giving up something precious to our sense of self. I will spend the rest of my life trying to convince anyone who is interested, that we don't need to give up one ounce of ourselves to understand another quite clearly and accurately. And in so doing, utterly destroy the need for conflict.

I am fully aware of how that sounds to most ears. I will not back down.

www.ingramcontent.com/pod-product-compliance
Lightning Source LLC
Chambersburg PA
CBHW061531250726
48657CB00005B/2179